Diarrhea of the Mouth

Kimberly Jones

BookLeaf
Publishing

India | USA | UK

Presentation by *BookLeaf Publishing*

Web: www.bookleafpub.com

E-mail: info@bookleafpub.com

ISBN: 9789360941581

First edition 2024

To:

My Mother Vergie Best, for birthing me with the wit and knowledge that spans generations.

My Spiritual Mother Sophia Baldwin, your accuracy, love, and wisdom is exactly what I need when I need it.

My Ayden Middle school teacher, Sandy Matthews for caring enough to recognize my gift.

My 30 year Best Friend Ericka Williams-we're loc'd in forlife and longer,

My Rise n Thrive Community 2.0 -my book is a result of our manifestations..thanks!

My 20 plus year "Bestie" Latesha Farrow for pushing and believing in me when I didn't believe in myself.

My Attorney Thomas "Daequan" Sherman for teaching me my worth and to double it while adding tax!

My cheerleaders Melody Allen & Victoria Higgs your support is everything.

My cousin Cora Taft-it's simply something special about Jones Blood,

My good sis Janice Westbrook-your loyalty can never be questioned, our secrets ARE still secrets.

My AYDEN, NC - ALLEN DRIVE family for reminding me there's no place like OUR place.

My KUXZIN Tyesha Pinkston for always answering, always positive, always with the shits-Thank U

MY DIVADANCE Sandy Springs family-it's the CONFIDENCE for me.

My Dance Instructor/Therapist @theofficialdreakelly
..thanks for the reminder to let her go, so I can grow.

My siblings Natalie Ward, Katie Taylor, Carol Jones,
Cheryl Jones, Jeff Jones, James Earl Jones, Mitch Best- I

will ALWAYS be your lil sister whether you like it or not...
WE FOREVER..

ACKNOWLEDGEMENT

I didn't tell anyone I was writing this book. However, if you've ever liked or read my poetry and supported me in anyway-This book is for you.

PREFACE

This book was written for anyone who's ever been misunderstood..

BREAKUPS 2 MAKEUPS

We've broken up, gotten back together, more
times than it was worth-
I still would give you chance after chance and
all you gave me was hurt.
Coming to my senses, gaining some strength &
in the process of clearing my mind-
There are some things, I must address and now
seems the right time.
Thank you for all the terrible insults and saying I
was of no use-
Thank you for saying how unattractive I was and
the rest of the verbal abuse,
Straight from the salon, hair and nails done, you
always let me know-
The moments I had the most confidence-you
called me Bitch or Heaux.
I asked myself, why did I stay the relationship
was no fire just smoke-
Now I see you, for who you really
are-insensitive, unappreciative, a joke.
Nothing can stop me, not the luck of the Irish or
even a four leaf clover-
If It wasn't before, iT truly is now, and IT my
friend is Over.

SHATTERED

In my mind I picture exactly how it would be-
The day you took the blinders off and finally
recognized me.
I thought it'd be at the bar, or was that wishful
thinking-
Maybe you'd approach sexy as fuck-and ask
what I was drinking.
Tell me you've been checking me out, really
liked my smile-
Or compliment what I was wearing, really
digging my style.
No matter when I saw you, I knew just what I'd
say-
It didn't matter when it would be, was prepared
either way.
I must admit, when you walked in, I was stunned
more like surprised-
I was glad to have been already in line-hiding
my face and my eyes.
Excited for you to see this version of me-from a
3 to a four leaf clover-
The moment I've waited for so long, was here
and almost over.
I could smell your cologne, growing stronger
with every step-

You got in line, right behind me-I swear I could
feel your breath.
You then touched me on my shoulder, and spoke
with a sexy whisper-
You said 'Hi Kim, thought that was you, and
ahh, what's up with your Sister?'

LESSON LEARNED

The only person in life you can change is U-
You can't control other people no matter what
you do.
If you're in a committed relationship, but in
Love alone-
Just let go, in your heart you know this person's
gone.
So many times we endure and fight as hard as
we can,
You can not make a Heaux a housewife, & you
can't take the mouse out the man.
It's human nature to be empathetic, we all
should possess that trait-
Walking a mile in someone else's shoes is a
journey we all should take.
That mile you walk may be tough, but you'll
make it with little surprise-
Maybe just maybe it'll touch your heart as well
as open your eyes.
If you come away unaffected and feeling just the
same-
Don't get mad or lose your cool, you have
yourself to blame.

ITS OK NOT TO BE OK

Sometimes I want to run, sometimes I want
to scream-
I try to wake myself up, it's reality not a dream.
Sometimes I need hugs, sometimes I need
reassurance-
I truly need a little more strength, a little more
endurance.
Sometimes I'm ecstatic, sometimes
I'm depressed-
I know I deserve so much more, at times settle
for less.
Sometimes I hold on, sometimes I let go-
In situations I've said yes, I should've just said
no.
Sometimes things work for the best, other times
it's the other way-
Just know in either of these events it's ok to not
be OK.

The Nerve

You never cease to amaze me, even after
knowing you for so long-
You've convinced yourself that you are right,
but you couldn't be more wrong.
Bringing you food, so you could eat, always
going out on a limb.
Catching you cheating, the verbal abuse, I held
on but you strayed-
So many times, wanting to give up, instead I
fought and prayed.
Now you tell me, you've met someone else and
that you're conversating.-
Translate that in lamens terms-you have
someone new you're dating.
This puzzles me, if this is so, and you said this
was the case-
Where was she, just like last week, when we
fucked all over your place?
Remember my thighs, clenched your waist,
I rode you till you had spasms-
Feeding your ego, I said yes, it was
No-pretending to have orgasms.
I guess I'm in awe, of how quick, you're moving
on with another-

But as you know that works both ways-a dime a
dozen are lovers.
Rose petal massages, candlelit dinners, limo's
ain't it funny-
Amazing sex with no regrets-you had it all you
dummy.
You claim there's nothing like new pussy and if
in fact its true-
What's done and old in your eyes, to the next
man is new.

KARMA

There once was a time you were all I desired-
Attention and respect were the gifts I required.
I thought loving you enough would make
everything ok-
But loving you wasn't enough to me want to
stay.
As the problems begin to surface, of course
you'd blame me-
But how do you blame someone else for your
own insanity?
No hugs in the morning or kisses good night it
all became so routine-
After making love, if you call it that, you'd get
yours and get up, now thats mean.
Wanting you to hold me, hold me close, you'd
always pull away-
I never ever pressed the issue, cause every dog
has his day.
Through it all we stayed together and to you
everything is fine-
I don't know whether you're comfortable or
maybe to dam blind.
In short- you don't make me feel, like you use
to-
That's exactly why i've been cheating on you.

NIGHT NIGHT

Acknowledging your errors are qualities of a
Man-
Even if you can't admit to me to yourself you
can.
How do you fix such huge errors or correct such
grand mistakes-
Warned you about tainting truth and tempting
the hand of fate.
Moves you made to prove your point, were so
harsh and deep-
Now the bed U made out there-is calling you to
sleep.

FUCK DEPRESSION

Have you ever felt so defeated-
Completely exhausted, energy depleted?
Beaten down by thoughts of old-
Hurting mind, body, and soul?
That's when you truly gotta dig deep-
Fight the woes and the sleep.
Wipe the tears, fix your face-
Change your energy, change your space.
Depression is something we all go through-
Just keep fighting when it happens to you.

DON'T COME BACK

Don't come back when you realize the grass over
there wasn't green-
I wouldn't have you back if you bathed in Clorox
or gargled with Mr. Clean.
Not knowing the insecure person you were, or
the selfish person you'd be-
Or the basket case I'd become as a result of you
dating me.
Petite, slender, feminine-target of all your hits-
Every insult, any insult would start and end with
Bitch.
Although my body may ache for you, in
translation my mind is lost-
My soul's the only part-that makes sense-and it's
telling you to Fuck Off.

FRIENEMIES

Thank you for the friendship, I did not see it
coming-
Cause if I did I would've hid or probably took
off running.
I never would've believed it, was always there
for you-
As soon as you're upset with me, the first thing
that you do.
Run and tell my business, and with who I slept-
Meanwhile, I'm over here making sure all your
secrets kept.
Although we'll never break any bread-nor laugh
or hug or talk-
Thank you so much for showing me, even
Snakes can walk.

COMING OUT

We've always run into each other, I never gave
you the time-
You never even peaked my interest, never
crossed my mind.
I was around you more than most because of our
mutual friends-
Could smell you coming a mile a way, and
completely ignore you then.
I made up my mind that I wanted you, kinda
craved you all along-
Just didn't know how to approach you, you came
on so very strong.
The day that I pulled you, changed my life-I'll
never be the same-
I'm in Love with a woman, they call her Mary
Jane.

MAMA

Responsible for so many fears- Wiped my ass
and my tears.
Rather have peace over any drama- No one else
but my MAMA!

New School Year-5 new pants & shirts-
7 days a week, sometimes she worked.
Her own childhood filled with Trauma- She's a
Overcomer, that's my MAMA!

Fighter, Lover, SuperAchiever- Sassy, Classy,
Dynamic Libra. Good deed doer, believer in
Karma
Defying all odds, yes that's my MAMA!

Taught me the game and how it's played, The
reason I was 19, before I got laid- Protective
like, secret service for Obama- Our 1st lady,
that's My MAMA!

MCM

My MCM today is to recognize no other-
So how about a round of applause for those
"Down LOW Lovers"
I have many Bisexual and Gay friends also
Family-
But it's you, filled with untruth-who seems most
confused to me.
You're fine enough to attract women, and YES,
honey you do-
But you seem to fail to mention-YOU also date
MEN too.
You're so masculine, and so hard, not to mention
your voice-
When it comes to dating do's-give these people a
choice.
Stop gambling with these peoples lives, or said
better yet-
You'e playing a very dangerous game,
something like Russian roulette.
You don't have to heed these words, nor do you
have to listen-
Just know whenever it hits the fan, you'll
probably come up missing.

VIOLATED

It was my 30th bday, we more than celebrated,
About 10 of my girls at my besties place-I felt
appreciated.
We headed out to the club, having fun is what I
was thinking-
Never could hold my liquor, but tonight I said
"I'm drinking."
After a few hours and about 5 drinks I said
"Bestie I'm fucked up"-
The club was about to close, she said 'you had
enough".
Stumbling outside, they had to carry me,
eventually put me in the car-
They knew I was in no condition to drive, and
since my bestie didn't stay far-
My 10 plus friends went back to her place and
carried me up the stairs-
I was blacking out but could hear voices, I knew
exactly who was there.
They put me in my besties bed, she climbed in
and fell asleep too-
At least I was safe and sound, and that's all I
really knew.
Not knowing how long I've been sleep I felt
what felt like sex-

Struggling to sober up-imagine what was next.
I could feel the thrust of a body, as I constantly
blinked my eyes-
Trying to gain clarity and focus beyond my
cries.
Finally eyes wide open, alert I soon discovered-
Right then in that very moment-I was being
fucked by her brother.
I pushed him off, ran to the bathroom, sick,
nauseated, that Bum-
As I sat down to pee, out came this Monsters
cum.
When I came out, he sat in a chair, you could see
the rage on my face-
My bestie came out of her room, I felt so
disgraced.
"How did I end up on the couch, thought I was
in your bed?"—
Her bf came in the middle of the night-and they
put me on the couch instead.
Not thinking about her lurking brother, filled
with envy and hate-
If I knew nothing else, I knew I had been raped.

BAE

You walked into my life, like a breath of fresh
air,
Attentive, overwhelming and messing up my
hair.
Your timing is so perfect, I love the vibes you
bring-
Yes of course I'll marry you, I'm engaged to
SPRING!

BE ALRIGHT

I can't lie and say it doesn't hurt, to see you with
another-
Til I realized what I was losing an abusive 10
minute brother.
You look so comfy with your new boo-or is that
just pretend-
Trying to get a rise out of me to hurt me once
again?
For your new girl, I have instructions, you
probably should come with a sign-
Selfish ass man, Mama's Boy, a complete waste
of time.
Doesn't know where he's going, has no sense of
direction-
2 minutes of him on his back, is how you'll
receive affection.
Never ever argue back, cause he will yell and
swear-
You've disrespected his manhood-which means
you just don't care.
Beware of the puppet like behavior, he's
controlled by another,
No I'm not talking about his friends, I'm talking
about his Mother.

She'll help him cheat, she'll cover his lies, she'll
condone what he do-
All while smiling in your face, confessing her
love for you.
One more thing, to keep in mind, while you
think your winning-
A leopard can not change his spots he only
changes his women.

CHANGES

The first six months of the relationship is the
honeymoon stage-
Saying and doing all the right things no time to
misbehave.
After that reality sets in, to a drunk its like
getting sober-
In other words, fuck what you heard, the party is
indeed over.
Conversation turn to comments-feelings they use
to hide-
Boxer shorts turn to briefs-it's sexual suicide.
The person you were when we met is the person
I need you to be-
That creative, sexy, individual-pursuing the hell
outta me.
Healthy relations and strong couples do indeed
make me tingle-
They're far and few and I'm happy for you-but
for me-I'm single.

WHY

Why do you think because I wear weave I must
not have any hair-
Why do you think, if you ask me to dinner, the
tab we're supposed to share?
Why do you think, if we have sex night one, I
must be a hoe or a trick-
Why do you think, if you go down on me, I'll
reciprocate and suck your dick?
Why do you think, if you have a tattoo, bikers
I'll automatically like-
Why do you think, a woman with a tongue ring,
must be a freak or a dyke?
Why do you think, if we chat on the net,
eventually we'll meet-
Why do you think, because I'm skinny, I'm
bulimic, anorexic, or don't eat?
Why do you think, me walking by, is an
invitation to grab my ass-
Why do you think, because you date me now,
you can judge my past?
Why do you think, I can't be pleased no matter
how hard I try-
Why do you think, the only answers to these
questions are not answers it's just WHY?

TAKE IT OFF

If I take away your jewelry, watches, chains and
rings-
Got rid of all your fancy cars dam near
everything.
Would anyone still listen, do you think you'd be
heard-
Would anyone walk around quoting your every
word?
Are you strong enough to stand alone-resting
solely on you-
Or are you the mouse, behind the man, lost
within the crew?
Do you have what it takes to move the crowd,
can you really roc the mic-
Are you really a bad MC or basically all hype.
What exactly would it take, respect you'd
have to gain-
Would you lose all that pizazz, can you rely on
your name?
Not many people can stand on their will, but
those that can and do-
Will always remain on the top, make sure that
person is you.

BYE BYE

Why is it when I think I'm over you, you show
up or come around-
That brick wall of strength, to keep you away,
you somehow just tear down.
You smile at me, say a few nice words in your
arms I always go running-
Enjoyed last time, cause I've made up my
mind-next time I won't be coming.
You wanted your freedom, you chose your boys,
in short you wanted to play-
Those streets you fought so hard to run-is where
your ass will stay.
Bragging rights for having my body-skill, no
that's luck-
What meant so much to you, meant nothing to
me-it was a charity fuck.
Don't get me wrong, I know that you know me,
and yes I know that you care-
But have you forgotten how selfish I am, a man I
will not share.
That in and out of my life, whenever you want,
as if I'm a revolving door-
You've been cut off and cut short that path exists
no more.

When you see me, don't even speak, and
remember this last verse-
You can never ever truly play a player, cause the
player is gonna play you first.

* 9 7 8 9 3 6 0 9 4 1 5 8 1 *